TIME FOR POETRY

TIME FOR POETRY

POEMS FROM THE LITERATURE AND
WRITING MAGNET CLUSTER SCHOOLS

CHICAGO PUBLIC SCHOOLS
IN PARTNERSHIP WITH
CHICAGO PARK DISTRICT

EDITED BY STEPHEN YOUNG, FRED SASAKI
PAGE HUBBEN AND SHEILA KEELEY

PUBLISHED BY THE POETRY FOUNDATION

Coverdesign by Winterhouse Studio, www.winterhouse.com.
Cover and event photographs by Brook Collins, Chicago Park District
    photojournalist.
Back cover art by Tatiana S., Burbank Elementary School.

WWW.POETRYFOUNDATION.ORG

POETRY

FOUNDATION

The Poetry Foundation is an independent literary organization committed to a vigorous presence for poetry in our culture. It exists to discover and celebrate the best poetry and to place it before the largest possible audience.

To our teachers
who make time rich

CONTENTS

Time for Poetry

ACKNOWLEDGMENTS

This project in all of its phases would not have been possible without the great enthusiasm and measureless contributions of Chicago Park District Commissioner Cindy Mitchell, Julia Bachrach, Chicago Park District Historian, and Melissa Cook and Jack Spicer of the Fountain of Time Committee. Special thanks are due to many Chicago Park District staff members, including Elizabeth Milan, A.J. Jackson, Caroline O'Boyle, Denise Reed Burbon, Jaqui Ulrich, Michelle Jones, Jessica Faulkner, Erin Swanborn, Janie Collins, Brook Collins, Carla Mayer, Tom Schorsch, and Beverly Napier. Brenda Palm of the Parkways Foundation was instrumental in coordinating the June 7th recitation, while Nora Brooks Blakely, Sonya Malunda, Jeff McCarter, Linda Wing, Eric Taylor, Kapoot Clowns, Zahara Baker, Full Effects Dance Company, stiltwalkers from CircEsteem, Yaya Kabo on drums, and the Chocolate Chips Theater made it entertaining and memorable. The Hyde Park Herald, Seminary Co-op Bookstores, Powell's Bookstores, University National Bank, Hyde Park Bank, and the University of Chicago provided financial support and publicity.

Chicago Public School teachers and administrators deserve deep gratitude, especially the Office of Academic Enhancement, Chicago Public Schools. Interns Sarah Gilligan and Kelly Daly helped prepare the manuscript, while Nancy Diaz and Jeanette Alfaro translated poems composed in Spanish. Finally, cheers to all the kids who by writing and reciting poems remind us that it's always time for poetry.

The Paradox of Time

Time goes, you say? Ah no!
Alas, Time stays, we go;
Or else, were this not so,
What need to chain the hours,
For Youth were always ours?
Time goes, you say?—ah no!

Ours is the eyes' deceit
Of men whose flying feet
Lead through some landscape low;
We pass, and think we see
The earth's fixed surface flee:—
Alas, Time stays,—we go!

Once in the days of old,
Your locks were curling gold,
And mine had shamed the crow.
Now, in the self-same stage,
We've reached the silver age;
Time goes, you say?—ah no!

Once, when my voice was strong,
I filled the woods with song
To praise your "rose" and "snow";
My bird, that sang, is dead;
Where are your roses fled?
Alas, Time stays,—we go!

See, in what traversed ways,
What backward Fate delays
The hopes we used to know;
Where are our old desires?—
Ah, where those vanished fires?
Time goes, you say?—ah no!

How far, how far, O Sweet,
The past behind our feet
Lies in the even-glow!
Now, on the forward way,
Let us fold hands, and pray;
Alas, Time stays,—we go.

HENRY AUSTIN DOBSON

PREFACE

W. H. Auden famously wrote in his elegy for W. B. Yeats that "poetry makes nothing happen." Lorado Taft, one of Chicago's most celebrated sculptors, might have disagreed. In 1907, he explained "a vagrant line or two of Austin Dobson's once made a great impression on me. Says the poet: 'Time goes, you say? Ah, no! / Alas, Time stays, we go.'" What happened as a result of that impression is Taft's magnificent *Fountain of Time* sculpture, which graces the meeting point of Washington Park and the Midway Plaisance on Chicago's South Side.

Those stray lines from Dobson come from a poem called "The Paradox of Time." The work is reprinted here in full because it, along with Taft's sculpture, helped make the anthology you hold in your hands possible. Poetry does make things happen after all.

The Time for Poetry project, a collaboration among the Poetry Foundation, the Chicago Park District, and Chicago Public Schools Literature and Writing Magnet Cluster Program began in March, when over a hundred teachers gathered for a day's worth of workshops about poetry and public art. Among the very talented presenters were representatives from Young Chicago Authors, the Poetry Center of Chicago's Hands on Stanzas Program, poet and author John O'Connor, Harlee Till, Sheila Keeley, Melissa Cook, Carla Mayer, Julia Bachrach and Cindy Mitchell. Back in their classrooms, the teachers asked their 3rd- through 8th-grade students to write poems about time and the sculpture. Collected here is just a small sample of the thousands of poems submitted, all of which will be put in a time capsule to be installed inside the *Fountain of Time* when the sculpture is rededicated.

But the consequences of Dobson's poem don't end there. On June 7, 2005, over two thousand school children gathered at the *Fountain of Time* to recite poetry and draw attention to a landmark sculpture in need of restoration. If poetry helped inspire the sculpture, perhaps it can help save it. In addition to "The Paradox of Time," the students delivered verses by two of Chicago's greatest poets—Carl Sandburg and Gwendolyn Brooks—and in this mass recitation, they were lucky enough to be led by Nora Brooks Blakely, who, like her mother the poet, has worked tirelessly to make better lives for Chicago's kids through art.

The Time for Poetry event was a bright and joyous realization of the Poetry Foundation's mission to help foster a vigorous presence for poetry in our culture. On June 7th one could even call that presence boisterous. Lorado Taft once observed that humankind is distinct from other animals by our ability to create art, and thus speak to future generations. Poetry's first function, several millennia ago, was to tell history and in telling history, it helped give rise to civilization. We continue to recite our common heritage in order to keep communities together. The young voices collected here will speak to generations still to come, but they may also speak to adults, the generation not gone yet, but gone a little further along time's constant gaze.

STEPHEN YOUNG
PROGRAM DIRECTOR
THE POETRY FOUNDATION

INTRODUCTION

Like the diverse representations of humanity reflected in the Lorado Taft sculpture, the *Fountain of Time*, children from neighborhoods across the city came together in the spring of 2005 to celebrate their time—to write, to learn, to create. The Time for Poetry project served as a springboard for the students to publish and appreciate their own original poetry. The project also made it possible for children from different backgrounds to share knowledge and experience while becoming familiar with such renowned poets as Carl Sandburg and Gwendolyn Brooks.

This publication is a celebration of the collaboration between the Chicago Park District, the Poetry Foundation, and the Chicago Public Schools Literature and Writing Magnet Cluster Program. The following poems are a compilation of selected works written by literature and writing students across grade levels and inspired by the *Fountain of Time* sculpture.

We are in deep appreciation for the opportunity presented by the Poetry Foundation for recognizing our students' work, bringing together the many resources that were open to all children, and providing an experience that will be rich in its rewards.

Finally, we thank our children for their insightful poetry and we express our gratitude for the dedicated, enthusiastic teachers who lead them in learning.

SHEILA KEELEY
ADMINISTRATOR
LITERATURE AND WRITING MAGNET CLUSTER SCHOOLS
CHICAGO PUBLIC SCHOOLS

Time

In the beginning there were Adam and Eve
They multiplied and multiplied until they made me
The music changed from jazz to hip hop
All forms of expression
From punk to Usher's Confessions
The 10th century to the 21st
From my great grandma to my mom...all different generations
To be different is a great sensation
People are old and people are young
From worshiping to speaking in tongue
Time passes and the future is near
The next generation we can hear
We're young now but we get old
We're soon to have young things to be told
We had good times but now we leave it to...
The next generation.

Janyce C.
DE DIEGO COMMUNITY ACADEMY

Time!

I only have a minute,
Only 60 seconds in it
It's forced upon me
Can't refuse it
Didn't think it
Didn't choose it
But it's up to me to use it
Punish me if I abuse it
Just a tiny little minute
But eternity is in it.

Leonard M.
KOZMINSKI COMMUNITY ACADEMY

Poem of Time

Time is something
you won't forget.
You'll remember something
and you'll regret.
You remember things
that come out of the dark,
like eating ice cream
at the park.

You're like a flower.
Each day you live,
a petal falls.
And when the last petal falls,
you fall.

Salmaan H.
SOLOMON ELEMENTARY SCHOOL

Untitled

Day turns to night before night turns to day
The eternal journey began, the road went one way
Only to drop us off will it stop, though its journey goes on
Progressing in place, the cycle moves on
Only our eyes see the crossroads, as goes a life
After life, the same is for all but for time
'Tis the age of progression, the reign stays eternal
Eternal, time's reign, but life's not immortal
With eyes we see the aging of all life and the sands of time
Deception, the sand is still as we move, time won't rewind
We move only forward. Wise to wisely be wise.

Felipe B.
CHAVEZ ELEMENTARY SCHOOL

Stuck

I want to be
little again
and be known as a kid
be so small
I can't always
open the pickle jar lid
play in the park
and skin my knee
slide down the slide
yelling wee wee wee
I want to be stuck
and be a kid
for all time
where daddy tucks
me in bed
and sings me a
lullaby rhyme

Amber R.
MOOS ELEMENTARY SCHOOL

Time

Time is priceless. It is our life.
But some take it away with a gun or a knife.
Sometimes it can go very fast,
And sometimes you'll think it forever lasts.
Believe it or not, we have a small period of time.
Our bodies will pass over, both yours and mine.
So don't put this precious time to waste.
It holds your life and your fate.

Elyah O.
ALCOTT ELEMENTARY SCHOOL

Time

I wish I could live again
I wish I could stop the time
To make two dreams come true that
I didn't do when I was alive.

Rocio B.
PILSEN COMMUNITY ACADEMY

Time!!!

Why do a crime when you can't do the time?
When you're in jail you turn pale.
Don't follow that trail cause you will only fail.
In jail you eat slime because you did a crime.
I'm Mrs. Time. I hate doing crimes
because you eat slime in jail then you turn pale.
Time is your life. Remember that!!!

Jordan M.
G. WASHINGTON ELEMENTARY SCHOOL

From Then to Now

A child lost in life.
No one there to find him.
From violence and gangs,
To sex and drugs,
These kinds of things to guide him.
From then to now he looks at his life,
Wondering how he came to this.
Look at my flaws,
The broken laws.
Now I see,
What I have come to be.

The pain I've caused,
The line I've crossed.
From then to now I see it all,
The light has flashed above me.
From then to now I'll never be the same.
From now on I'll be a better person.
Life has truly changed.

Jennifer M.
MOOS ELEMENTARY SCHOOL

Time

Future
Destiny, outcome
Up, forward, clockwise
Time, date, when, now
Do-over rewind, counter clockwise
Old, wrinkly
Past

William S.
ALCOTT ELEMENTARY SCHOOL

Time

Children wanting to get older; wiser,
Thinking life is so slow.

Wanting to grow up,
Get away,
But having nowhere to go.

But they should wait,
Save their time,

Because at least I know,
Time is a precious thing.

So we should wait,
To grow.

Charlene C.
CLAY ELEMENTARY SCHOOL

Barbies

Barbies will
never change.
They will always
stay the
same.

Their feet will always
be small.
Their hair will never
grow.

They will always
stay the
same.

But I may change.

Molly G.
MITCHELL ELEMENTARY SCHOOL

Times Goes By

My favorite Barbie turns into my favorite CD
Time flies like a butterfly
My favorite CD turns into my favorite sweater
Time flies like a butterfly
My favorite sweater turns into my favorite walking cane
Time flies like a butterfly
But I don't want to fly by to leave my favorite things.

Rosa C.
G. WASHINGTON ELEMENTARY SCHOOL

Life Goes

It's been a long time
since I saw her. I
miss her. She is a
wonderful person.
Want to know who she
is? My mom!

I saw her in December.
It wasn't long enough,
but I wouldn't change
those days for anything.

I wish I could have
more time, but I
guess that is how
life goes. It doesn't
tell you when your
time is up.
It just
goes.

Karol L.
CHAVEZ ELEMENTARY SCHOOL

Time

Time begins for us as a glimmer in our mother's eye as we emerge as
Infants into a mysterious world so new and cold
   we continue on our life journey,
Maturing daily and discovering life's triumphs
   and trials until that day when,
Eternity begins a new journey for our destiny.

Anonymous
KOZMINSKI COMMUNITY ACADEMY

Time Is Unpredictable

Time is like the dream that hasn't been dreamed.
Time is like the book that hasn't been read.
Time is like the food that hasn't been eaten.
Time is like the war that hasn't been beaten.
Time is precious and tends to be measured
   and should be treated like a treasure.
Today time is cloaked in mystery.
Tomorrow, time is history!

Karina
MOOS ELEMENTARY SCHOOL

Let's Ride on the Wings of Time

As little kids, we run free.
We have nothing to do. Our lives are easy.

As big teenagers, it's all work and chores,
and we have no time to play outdoors.

As adults, work is really rough,
but we have to stand tall and be very tough.

As grandparents our lives are easy again,
we have to teach little ones and try to be their friends.

Antiara T.
BURBANK ELEMENTARY SCHOOL

Time

Time, time it's so slow.
It stabs you in the heart
and eats your soul.
It never stops to say hello,
it zips by and says *go, go, go*.
Me and others agree,
Time is cool and everyone likes me.
Everyone likes father time,
Me and him like to eat pie.
MMMM...pie.

Ethan
SOLOMON ELEMENTARY SCHOOL

Clock, Clock

Clock, clock, please
Stop, you're too fast.

This day is so nice,
To play soccer in
   The park.

Clock, clock, please
Stop you're too fast.

Please don't take

Stephnie
wndme

This day, I don't
Have enough time
 To play.

So clock, clock, please
Stop, you're too fast.

Tick, tock, tick, tock.
Please clock, why won't
 You stop?

Yesenia F.
CHAVEZ ELEMENTARY SCHOOL

Time

Tick tock
the time goes by.
I stand here wondering why,
Why everything all of a sudden changes?
And why everything has to rearrange.
It feels like I am cold on the inside and warm on the outside.
I need to find a way to somehow confide
Why is it that lately the world is falling apart?
Once it falls apart you feel lost and you have no idea where to start.
I don't understand how everything went from right to wrong.
It's like you want time to go slow, but then it takes too long.
Tick tock
the time goes by.
I stand here wondering why,
Why does everything have to come to an end?
It's like in one day you gain one, and then again you lose a friend.
You feel hurt, and then you don't.
Your heart wants to cry but then it won't.
Everything is twisted, but yourself is the one you cannot find.
It's like a tornado, but it's not reality, it's in your mind.
Don't you remember...when you were five and running around
    eating popsicles,

And you had nothing to worry about except Barney and Teletubbies.
And as time went by, you became older and your whole life was filled
    with nothing but worries.
Tick tock
the time goes by.
I stand here wondering why,
Why is it when you don't want to grow up, you do.
And when you do, sometimes you feel like you can't be you.
You feel different, like another person, but you still can't figure out
    why,
Then you realize, it's a reality check, it's the truth and not a lie.
There are many times when you want to give up, not just on life but
    on everything.
But before giving up, think twice, because in one minute, you can go
    from having everything to nothing.
Tick tock
the time goes by.
I stand here wondering why,
Why the time goes slow when we want it to go fast, and why it goes
    fast when we want it to go slow.
Tick tock
Tick tock
Tick tock
The time it just keeps on going and never stops!

Megha S.
G. ARMSTRONG ELEMENTARY SCHOOL

Enough Time

What happened to life when time was good,
and everything and everybody really understood?
When life went on no matter what
and only time could tell when to start and finish stuff.
Time is very important always and everywhere,
it helps to leave or to stay somewhere.
No matter what you are doing, something good or wrong,
but hurry because before you know it time is gone.

So try to finish through sun and rain,
or sometimes you feel happiness or sometimes you feel pain.
Just as you start to begin and your brain really erupts,
you get going then ding... Time's Up!!!!!

Cassata M.
SCHILLER ELEMENTARY SCHOOL

Time

Your life is like time,
your time is counted
for it knows when you
die.

Your life is like time,
for you see the light
every day and when you
don't know it you may
not see light again.

Your life is like time,
for your life on earth is
for a while, and then you
go to heaven.

Eugenio R.
CASTELLANOS ELEMENTARY SCHOOL

What about Time

Time is life
life is about time,
it goes forward only
but once behind
"daylight saving time."

Whatever you do or say
it's said and done,
at points time is boring
at points time is fun.

You want time to fly
because you want this,
you want it to go slow
because that's something you
just can't miss.

Time has the same rhythm—
it's not fast, it's not slow.
Wherever time ticks that's
where life goes.

James M.
CHAVEZ ELEMENTARY SCHOOL

Awaiting

A season when it's sad and cold
In a day you want it to be summer
Just hoping it was that day
Glaring at the sun
Beaming down a white door
Awaiting the snow to melt as
    salt
    all
    soggy

Seeing the wind blow the leaves
Off the summer trees!
Watching the people shiver their way home
Feeling the breeze down to their toes
But, winter takes a long time
so why not enjoy it!

Anna D.
PILSEN COMMUNITY ACADEMY

Untitled

Goodbye winter, snowflakes, ice, cold weather.
Hello spring, tulips, roses, sunflowers.
Goodbye spring, flowers and windy weather.
Hello summer, breezy weather, kids playing, pretty sights.
Goodbye school work, reading, math and science.
Hello summer vacation, swimming and barbeques.
Goodbye fifth grade, easy work, less work.
Hello sixth grade, hard work, more work.
Goodbye old ways, being bad and giving attitude.
Hello new ways, being good, and paying gratitude.

Angelica B.
POPE ELEMENTARY SCHOOL

I Remember

I remember when I was eight and going out on dates.
I remember when I was nine and wasting all my time.
I remember when I was ten and wanted to win.
I remember when I was eleven, wishing I could go to heaven.
I remember when I was twelve and thought I was going to fail.
I remember when I was thirteen, thinking I was fourteen.
I remember when I was fourteen, still wishing I was thirteen.

Matthew N.
POPE ELEMENTARY SCHOOL

Time

Forever moving
Like the river flows,
Growing older
As the great oak.

A gift so priceless
More than gold,
Nothing can possess.

Blowing past
Your closed eyelids,
Open them
And you see you're now old.

Memories are held more dear
The wiser you grow,
With its gentle touch
the whisper of age.

A healer
That can haunt,
Forgetfulness it mocks
The forever passing.

Samira K.
KILMER ELEMENTARY SCHOOL

Time

Time goes by fast.
We don't even realize it.
Times goes by like a blink of an eye.
Times goes by fast like a train on the tracks.
Time goes by so fast we don't even realize.

Jasmine E.
KOZMINSKI COMMUNITY ACADEMY

Lorado Taft at work on the *Fountain of Time*, circa 1922. The Time for Poetry event was planned to raise funds and awareness for conservation of the sculpture.

Students gather behind the *Fountain of Time* to rehearse "Jane Addams" and "Speech to the Young" by Gwendolyn Brooks, "The Paradox of Time," by Henry Austin Dobson, and "I Am the People, the Mob," by Carl Sandburg.

Father Time presides over 100 figures at different stages of life. While the sculpture figures have been restored, the reflecting basin remains in need of conservation.

Stiltwalking Father Time greets students.

Life

You live and you die
People are afraid of death
I'm not afraid

Living my life I'm free
Here it's a beautiful place
Living my life

Here it is coming
Death, should I be afraid?
No, because I lived

Danilla H.
WHITE ELEMENTARY SCHOOL

Time

Time
Slow, fast
Passing, happening, wasting
The most precious gift
Life

Diana G.
BURBANK ELEMENTARY SCHOOL

Past, Present, Future

The past is so hard
For me to give it away
I want to keep it.

I always say that
There's no time like the present

This is my saying.

I will always smile
With a bright future of hope
I will smile so wide.

Ashley C.
WHITE ELEMENTARY SCHOOL

It's a Time for Everything

it's a time to play.
it's a time to stay.
it's a time to weep.
it's a time to sleep.
it's a time to get mad.
it's a time to get glad.
it's a time to run.
it's a time to have fun.
it's a time to read.
it's a time to achieve.

I just can't wait.
I waited too long
For my new contract cell phone.

Anton A.
SCHILLER ELEMENTARY SCHOOL

Waiting in Time

When I was in my mom's stomach my mom waited a long time.
She waited nine months.
First, I was tiny.
Then, I became bigger.
When I was hungry, I moved a lot.

My mom gave me food.
Then, I was in one position.
I moved in another position.
I always moved a lot.
I also waited a long time to be born.
Now here I am.
I am eight years old.
Thank you Mom for my life!

Elizabeth R.
BURBANK ELEMENTARY SCHOOL

Calendar Time

Continuously time goes around giving life, bringing death.
Among these people it never stands still and waits for no one.
Living flowers, chirping birds, animals playing in the field, living,
    learning.
Even at last, the world is full of life with the hope of never ending.
Now, though time is slowing down, trying to pass us by, and
Death is near, but we don't know when it will come.
An eternity passes by in only a second,
Revealing that our time is done.

Daria H.
KOZMINSKI COMMUNITY ACADEMY

The Clock

I hang around all day,
as people rush, as they
see me.
They use me everywhere,
without me people
wouldn't know when
to leave to school, to work

or when to do anything you
would want to do in life.
I never stop unless my
batteries run out. You
can't stop time. Almost
everyone says "the clock
is not my friend, but my
enemy" because I don't
go at their rate, but that's
me and you or anyone else
can't stop me or my friend time.

Roman O.
CLAY ELEMENTARY SCHOOL

Always Time

Time will always pass you by.
Sometimes you wish you could
make it go back.
Sometimes you wish you could
make it go forward.
Sometimes you just want
it to stop.
In ways you wish you could
control time,
but it is not possible.
You can only go with it.
Time can be great but,
in other ways it can be
unpleasant.
Time can be precious.
Time can be monstrous but, as
always, time will pass you by.

Isa A.
MOOS ELEMENTARY SCHOOL

Flying Time

Did you know,
That time flies?
I always wondered
How it flew.

It may fly high or low.
Or maybe even South or
North or
East or
Maybe even West.

It doesn't matter
Where it goes,
It just happens like that
When it passes around the world.

Sometimes time is so fast
And sometimes
It's very slow.

I wish it followed my command,
Which is that I want it to be
Either fast of slow
By the way it will make me happy!

Yesenia M.
MITCHELL ELEMENTARY SCHOOL

Time vs. Lazy Clock

Time is mad at Lazy Clock
And Lazy Clock is mad at Time.
"Change the time on your clock!"
screamed Time.
"No, change the time to what the clock shows!"
screams Lazy Clock.

Then all of a sudden
the world fast forwarded
And the whole world was gone!
That's what you get
when you mess with time!

Paige D.
ROGERS ELEMENTARY SCHOOL

El Reloj en la Luna

Del cielo cayó un reloj,
El niño lo encontró,
Pensando que era un balón;
Lo mandó hasta la Luna.
La Luna se asustó viendo que era un reloj;
El niño le explicó y le dijo a la Luna
¡El susto que se metió!

Alandra R.
BURBANK ELEMENTARY SCHOOL

The Clock in the Moon

From the sky fell a clock,
A child found it,
Thinking it was a balloon,
He sent it to the Moon.
The Moon was frightened seeing that it was a
    clock;
The child explained and he told the Moon
how it had frightened him!

Translation by Nancy Diaz and Jeanette Alfaro

Time

I'm in the clock crew and I'm okay.
I tick all night and I tick all day.
I have two hands, I'm having a ball
Because I've got no arms at all.
My big hand can move sixty minutes in one hour.
I'm the one with the strength and power.
My small hand isn't quite as fast;
if they were in a race,
it would come last.
It takes so long just to get around
(12 hours you know).
It's careful, small and slow.
Now meet my friends that help me tick tock,
half past, quarter past, quarter to and o'clock.

Clashanna H.
ALCOTT ELEMENTARY SCHOOL

The Time Poem

Ticking tocking turning
The life
Slowly
Passed
In the years

Kenyatta P.
ALCOTT ELEMENTARY SCHOOL

Time

Time goes fast
As we go slowly
There is no time
For us to do things
Time is something
We can't control
As time goes as fast
As we do ourselves
Time we need it
We can't waste it
On just anything
Time goes fast
As we go slowly
Why is it like that
I don't know

Dominique B.
KOZMINSKI COMMUNITY ACADEMY

A Hole in Time

You exist as you always have
Day in and out you go
Everything is peaceful at last
Until you realize you have no past.

A hole has opened and you are gone
Non-existent in this world
History has been twirled
And your memories, friends and even family
Know not of your existence.

What shall become of you?
Your life twisted and new
Nowhere to go and no one to trust
Just changed in a thrust.

A hole has opened and you are gone
Non-existent in this world
Everything is at rest
But you must pass this test.

Will the hole ever close?
Will you ever return?

Jonathon R.
ROGERS ELEMENTARY SCHOOL

Time: A Mysterious and Complex Beauty

Go ahead and think about it.
But Father Time has a lot of power, no doubt about it.
He has the power to do almost anything.
Who knows what the future will bring?
Time can go slow and even fly.
No one knows exactly how or why.

Time can heal wounds like no one can.
Father Time will heal better than any man.
It seems time passes way too soon.
One minute we see the sun, the next we see the moon.
So we should learn to stop and smell the flowers.
And to enjoy these precious hours.

Mary C.
CLAY ELEMENTARY SCHOOL

Father Time, Father Time

Father Time, Father Time
I'm afraid of time's change.
Father Time, Father Time
Is there something we could arrange?

Oh Father Time, Oh Father Time
I'm tired of this mess.
Oh Father Time, Oh Father Time
Is this a test?

Father Time, Father Time,
Why does the clock tick?
Father Time, Father Time
Why does the clock tock?

Oh Father Time, Oh Father Time
I'll hold my family together.
Oh Father Time, Oh Father Time
The future will be better.

Father Time, Father Time
How much time do we have left?
Father Time, Father Time
Limits life and death.

Brittany G.
WEST PULLMAN ELEMENTARY SCHOOL

Rhyme Time

When you're a child
You want time to last
And when you're an adult
You want your childhood past

Time, time
People say it moves fast
And some people say
Time will last

Time is precious
Not meant to be frittered away
Because time can't repeat
You can't go back to that day

That day when your childhood was over
When you turned 21
To me that's when
Your childhood was done.

Nicole D.
ALCOTT ELEMENTARY SCHOOL

Can't Wait to Go to Space

Can't wait. Can't wait. To go to outer
space. Can't wait to see all the planets
in their regular place. Jupiter, Saturn, Pluto
too. Except for Neptune, it makes me feel
blue. Can't wait. Can't wait to go to
outer space. Can't wait to see stars in
the night. Can't wait to travel to Mars to see
martians fight. Can't wait to go to
Mercury, oh it's very hot. Going to Pluto to
freeze up a lot. Can't wait to go to outer space.

Wayne G.
SCHILLER ELEMENTARY SCHOOL

Time Flies

Time flies—time goes
It's like the life of a rose
The time changes—sun becomes stars.
Does this happen on the planet Mars?

Mrs. Roth's Class
MOOS ELEMENTARY SCHOOL

Untitled

Goodbye winter.
Hello summer.
Goodbye third grade.
Hello fourth grade.
Goodbye 5 years old.
Hello 9 years old.
Goodbye Mrs. Palmore.
Hello Mrs. Boghosian.
Goodbye Addition.
Hello Division.

Angela B.
POPE ELEMENTARY SCHOOL

Time Sculpture

Time is like money,
Use it wisely and you will succeed.
You should treasure time.

Respect life and live
Do fun things with your lifetime
Try to stay healthy.

Have a house and kids
Then grandchildren and wrinkles
You're happy now, right?

A capsule keeps life
It keeps lifetime memories
Memories that last.

Lemonia M.
SOLOMON ELEMENTARY SCHOOL

The Time Poem

School and learning combines into one.
Everyone should have lots of fun.
Digging and searching for fossils and bones
Is great when you find some from Ancient Rome.

Ancient money, clothes, and books,
The clock is ticking, time to take a look
Where our Ancestors lived long, long ago.

Review history, review the books,
Review the time at the assembly line.
Time flies and it feels weird.
Time is life that you can not fear.
Present, past, and future
Are like a combination lock.
When you put them together,
It's like one big time traveling knot.

Don't be shocked about what you find
Because in time we would all
Be part of an assembly line.

Rachel G.
SCHILLER ELEMENTARY SCHOOL

Millennium of Time

The world has been
Through millenniums of time,
Filled with the memorable events.
All of the people
Who have come and gone
Are helpful with these events.
I've only been around for a moment,
Yet, I have a couple of comments.
I'm helpful to series of events.

Chelsea J.
WEST PULLMAN ELEMENTARY SCHOOL

Time Flies By

Time flies by,
You'll believe it when you see it with your own eyes.
We did though,
And we didn't even know
That time flies by.

Seconds, minutes, hours and days
Quickly they pass away.
It goes bit by bit
Now it's your turn to see it—
That time flies by.

We realized too late
That time will not wait.
Over time we debated
That we would not be elated
That time flies by.

In the end we must accept that time cannot be rewound
It is lost and can never be found.

I hope you can be aware
Or at least try to care
That time flies by.

Olatundun A.
KILMER ELEMENTARY SCHOOL

Life Life

Life, life goes by fast.
Believe in your God,
And your last will last.
Life, life, clothes and socks.
Your life circulates around the clock.
Life, life gives time to shop.
Go too fast and your life will stop.
Life, life sometimes rhymes.
Hurry up you're wasting your time.
Life, life everyday.
Follow me, I'll guide your way.
Life, life you are burning.
It's time for school, you start learning.
Life, life every year.
You and your family get into gear.
Life, life you are spending
Hurry up, your life is ending.

Raven B.
SCHILLER ELEMENTARY SCHOOL

Untitled

I can't wait for school to end
I can't wait for my team to win
I can't wait for all types of stuff
I can't wait I think I had enough
I can't wait for time to pass
I can't wait I won't last
I am so tired of waiting I can't wait I'm losing patience
So now that I'm all alone I thank God that time is gone.

Sabian H.
SCHILLER ELEMENTARY SCHOOL

Time

Time—
What is time?
Is it friend or family?
Or love and care?
Or is it the shiniest of
A puppy's hair?
But—
How should I know?
I'm only eleven
But—
One of these days
We will all go up to heaven
When we do, I'll figure it out
Time
Until that day,
Time is nothing, but
A word on a line.

Kendall M.
DRAKE ELEMENTARY SCHOOL

Time

Time is fast
Time is slow
Time has numbers 1—12
It has minutes
It has hours
But who cares,
It's just time

Khiara V.
DE DIEGO COMMUNITY ACADEMY

Time

I see you, but I don't
feel you

I hear you but I can't
listen to you

I want to hold you
but my arms are not open

I'm praying and I
hope you help me and the rest
of us.

Kevin B.
G. WASHINGTON ELEMENTARY SCHOOL

Past, Present and Future

What is past present and future? How does a new beginning start, how does an ending end? But when one lives their life, they live with faith, strength and gratitude. But when one's life is over they are past, no longer living, terminated. As time passes children are brought into this place called earth, but only time can tell what will happen next. Past present and future are three elements that one must live in. When they die they're past, when they are living they're present and when they get a real chance at life they're the future.

Andre M.
KOZMINSKI COMMUNITY ACADEMY

Time

Time by time I'm going to high school
By time I'm getting older
By time people start to get busy
But what time will it be
when people realize the world is coming to
an end.
What time will we see that tomorrow
isn't promised.
What time will it be
when we get together as one body?
Together as one person? Together as one? United?
It does take time
Not next time but this time!
Time, time, time!
Time is running out.

Gennie J.
CHALMERS ELEMENTARY SCHOOL

Round Like a Circle

Oh circle you're round
Just like a clock
I wish I could knock you
right out of your socks
Oh time won't you go go go

Andrew G.
CLAY ELEMENTARY SCHOOL

My Life Is Like a Clock

12:00 = I was born
1:00 = Going to kindergarten
2:00 = Going to high school
3:00 = Graduate college
4:00 = Become a millionaire
5:00 = Get married
6:00 = Have kids
7:00 = Kids going to kindergarten
8:00 = Kids going to high school
9:00 = Kids graduating college
10:00 = Kids get jobs
11:00 = Kids' parents die
12:00 = Kids become parents

Joey S.
BURBANK ELEMENTARY SCHOOL

Time

Time is like an hourglass.
It goes by so fast.
I'm only eleven years old,
And don't like clothes to fold.
As you are reading this, I am getting old.
I may even be cold.
Or I might be dead.
My hair is the color of dark lead.

Laith
SOLOMON ELEMENTARY SCHOOL

Time

My grandpa's hair is changing,
from shiny black to sparkling snow.

He was young
but now is old.

He may not last forever,
but the memory of our time together
will never go away.

Jeanie H.
BURBANK ELEMENTARY SCHOOL

Time

Time can last forever
But not for every day
You want to use your time
In every single way.

You have 24 hours
Every single day
But you don't know what will happen
So don't throw your time away.

I like to spend my time
Spending days with all my friends
I only have 6 hours and
I don't want them to end.

I wasted my time on homework
Complaining that I had so much
The end of this day is getting closer
And that end I can almost reach.

Hanna G.
ALCOTT ELEMENTARY SCHOOL

Last Day of School

Walking to school
Still very early
Getting to class,
It's barely 8:30!!

Finally, school starts
Day still going slowly by.
But, hopefully, when the kids come in
Time will fly by.

It's 20 after two now
The bell will ring any second.
It's now 25 after two
The bell's probably broken, I reckon.

It got very quiet,
It seemed as time stopped.
When suddenly, we heard

The bell go, ¡RING!

Everybody laughed
And gave a loud cheer!
It finally came,
The last day of the school year.

Ana A.
BURBANK ELEMENTARY SCHOOL

Summer

Summer is my favorite season for only one reason. We're out of school and there are no more rules. We play until day breaks and sleep until the sun wakes. The only problem is it has to come to an end. Then I'll have the rest of my winter to spend in school.

Kalekey E.
KOZMINSKI COMMUNITY ACADEMY

School

School is tough
No matter what
All you do is try
If you try and fail
Ask the teacher to
Help you prevail
So take my advice not to fail,
But to prevail.

Melissa V.
G. WASHINGTON ELEMENTARY SCHOOL

Time Is Hard Work

Time is hard work,
you don't have that
much time. Enjoy
every moment, before
God takes you away. Don't
waste your time crying,
because you've made a mistake.
Get on with your life
and learn from them, because
time is wasting now.

Chaquale S.
KOZMINSKI COMMUNITY ACADEMY

Time

Time is our life
as it goes we grow
life goes on
but time just stays.
Use it wisely
because when you grow
you will know you go and time stays.
In the future you will see
that time really matters to you and me.
Without time we would not be here
and father time would have lots of tears.
In the future you will see
time makes us what we are to be.

Ryan H.
CLAY ELEMENTARY SCHOOL

Time Line

Life isn't a game.
It isn't always the same.
Remember those ancient times.
You used to make silly rhymes.
My life is mine.
I'm going to make it shine.
Make your own future great!
You can sometimes be late.
Life isn't about fame and fortune.
You can make your life shorten.
Just take it day by day.
Life will take you your way.
Don't forget your past
Because life will go by fast.
It can come to the very end
Where you can't defend.

Stephaun S.
SCHILLER ELEMENTARY SCHOOL

As Time Went By

As time went by, we couldn't even see,
how important, how successful, how simple life could be.
We gave up early, let obstacles get in the way,
we even gave up hope and let our dreams drift away.
We set our goals, and let ourselves seem so forgettable,
and let the little problems seem so unstoppable.
We could have worked towards our goals, and followed our hearts,
but instead, we gave up, let us and faith set apart.
Now, we can see how our lives turned out all because we didn't keep
that feeling we had from the start.
Life has changed so much of an abundance, it's so hard to describe,
who would have thought, who could have known,
that all of this could happen as time went by?

Alanna J.
KOZMINSKI COMMUNITY ACADEMY

Time

Time	Flying	It	No
is	at	moves	one
like	a	fast	knows.
a	shy	but	
fly	moment		

Emmy M.
SOLOMON ELEMENTARY SCHOOL

Time Is Very Tricky . . .

Time is very tricky
It can't be heard
Can't be felt
Can't be seen or touched
But yet you know it to be.

It changes and rearranges
Time sees, time learns
It sees life born and gone
Time can't be seen or touched
But yet you know it to be.

Time knows, time shows
Time knows truth, time knows a lie
Only time will tell you when you'll die.

Carolina P.
CASTELLANOS ELEMENTARY SCHOOL

It Is Never Late

Take a moment and think about the wrong things you have done.
It is never too late to make something right.
Make the bad and the wrong things turn into good and right things.
Everything has a moment to be changed.

Diana R.
ROGERS ELEMENTARY SCHOOL

Selfish Times

I had selfish times in my life.
When I was,
I lost my family, friends, and girlfriend,
and most importantly
I lost myself.

When I didn't walk my sister home,
She never talked to me again.
When I changed my personality,
to make myself look appealing,
My friends never talked to me again.
When I didn't share my feelings and thoughts,
My girlfriend didn't talk to me again.

What did I get out of these selfish times?
One thing
A person that I didn't even know
And that person was me.

Chris H.
ROGERS ELEMENTARY SCHOOL

Untitled

Goodbye to fighting.
Hello to the new me.
Goodbye night.
Hello morning.
Goodbye playing.
Hello work.
Goodbye doing bad.
Hello doing good.
It's good, good, good.

Elzine M.
POPE ELEMENTARY SCHOOL

Time

Time goes away and
my dad grows old and
that makes me go into
my room and think what
would I do when he
dies.
Time goes slow and
makes me think all
day when will I
get to see my grandma
again.
Time goes by and it makes
me think what would happen
with my future when I
grow sixteen.
When my dad took me cruising
with him that time made me
think what type of car would
he buy me.

Christian M.
CASTELLANOS ELEMENTARY SCHOOL

Time

Time is the color of a bumper
Time looks like endless numbers
Time tastes like peppers
Time smells like ash
Time feels like winter

Dominick G.
ALCOTT ELEMENTARY SCHOOL

Time

Tick tock the time is spring,
flowers are growing, grass is green,
the rivers are flowing, the leaves
on the trees are blowing, the
animals are nurturing one
by one in the forest.

Now spring has passed, it's
time to move on, as summer
will come with sunshine, and
blue skies, there may be raining
days as grass will grow and
animals may drink. How I love
summer days. From the
time I wake I hear the
birds singing to the evening,
I hear the owls hooting.
How I love the summer time.

Time will pass, the fall
will be here and animals
will be so snuggled deep in the woods.
Oh how time flies by.

Robert D.
G. WASHINGTON ELEMENTARY SCHOOL

Untitled

Time flies like a dragonfly
flies. Bees buzz like a chain saw
does. If only I could fly to be
above the sky to see my
family members that have died.
If only time didn't fly they
will still be alive, yes
time flies for the others.

Matthew
G. WASHINGTON ELEMENTARY SCHOOL

Time

To only turn back time
Would be as cheap as a dime
To change it one at a time
Would be such a great use of time
To have this one chance
We'd dance and prance
To only turn back time.

Alex
SOLOMON ELEMENTARY SCHOOL

Untitled

Perish	Gone	Future	Present	Past
Born	Live	Repeat	Remember	Change

Carolina P.
CASTELLANOS ELEMENTARY SCHOOL

There Was a Time

There was a time,
Where I was spoiled,
There was a time,
Where I was stubborn,
There was a time,
Where I would run and play until my blood would boil.
Now look at me,
The birds of time have flown,
I've grown older, taller,
I'm now 13,
I have new interests,
Such as reading, and writing.
I think of a day,
Where less sand is in my hourglass,
I'd have children,
A career in carpentry,
And perhaps, a love.
So then I'd sit upon my desk, and think
There was a time.

Vanessa M.
CASTELLANOS ELEMENTARY SCHOOL

Time is Going

Time is like the wind.
It goes past really fast.
One day you're really small.
The next, you're all grown up.

Spend your time wisely.
Try to be happy.
That's why you have to keep track of time
before your time runs out.

Javier M.
BURBANK ELEMENTARY SCHOOL

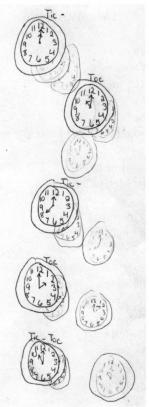

Krystal U.

G. WASHINGTON ELEMENTARY SCHOOL

Joshu C.

BURBANK ELEMENTARY SCHOOL

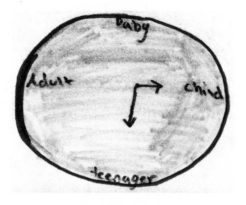

Danielle C.
KOZMINSKI COMMUNITY ACADEMY

Calvin V.
SOLOMON ELEMENTARY SCHOOL

The Hour of Time

Time does not end.
Time will be here
when you need it.
When you are alive
time won't hide and
whenever you want it
you will have it
whenever you want the
hours and the minutes
they will be there and
never end. When you
are growing you are
a baby. When you are
big you will be gone
and the time stays.

Ignacio M.
CHAVEZ ELEMENTARY SCHOOL

Time

Passing slowly, changing swiftly,
Time goes on and on.
It could be now, it could be later
but time is never wrong.
Simple numbers blinking, staring,
that you keep in mind.
Looking at your wrist impatiently
but it's only just the time.

Nakema J.
BURBANK ELEMENTARY SCHOOL

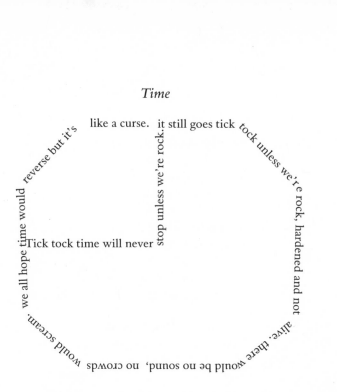

Tick tock time will never stop unless we're rock. like a curse. it still goes tick tock unless we're rock, hardened and not alive. there would be no sound, no crowds would scream. we all hope time would reverse but it's

Ajka K.
SOLOMON ELEMENTARY SCHOOL

Time

Time will always be by our side,
Time will always be in our lives,
Without time this world would change,
Without time it would be strange.
The only way we probably could tell time
Would be to look outside and see
Daylight or the moon
In the dark night.
What would happen
If we didn't have
     TIME?

Robert M.
DRAKE ELEMENTARY SCHOOL

The Time Poem

Time goes by so slow
Like the wind blows

Time sometimes goes by fast
It could maybe go blast-blast-blast

Time is the time of day
It just goes by so slow as some people say

Time is money, time is not play
It's something that goes by every other day

Time is slow, time is not fast
Time is just something that lasts

Robby C.
ALCOTT ELEMENTARY SCHOOL

It's Time! It's Time!

It's time! It's time!
To take a flight
on a plane during
the midnight.

It's time! It's time!
It is now noon,
I know I will see
the moon very soon.

It's time! It's time!
It's now time
for the sun
to rise and shine.

It's time! It's time!
It is now dawn,
I wake up and
give a big yawn.
It's time! It's time!

David F.
CASTELLANOS ELEMENTARY SCHOOL

What Is Time?

What is time?
Time is like a mime
It does not talk
It would not walk
It would not snooze
It moves
This is called time.

Tiffany D.
ROGERS ELEMENTARY SCHOOL

Time

Time
Steady, unsurpassed
Flying, Enduring, Passing,
Its destination—the future
Fate

Jonalyn O.
BURBANK ELEMENTARY SCHOOL

In the Life of Time

In the life of time
  There is a futuristic world
        You might want to go
In the life of time
  It is a reality world
In the life of time
  You can make wishes
        They may come true
In the life of time
  There is peace
        And harmony.
In the life of time
  There is love always
In the life of time
  There are many things
        You might want to do
In the life of time
  You could always laugh
        And be happy.
In the life of time
  You could just be a laid back
        Kind of person
IN THE LIFE OF TIME!

Matthew M.
DRAKE ELEMENTARY SCHOOL

Time

T is for Time, which I will spend
      Years of learning
      Getting the education
      To succeed in life.

I is for Ideal, which I will aim
      High to reach
      My goals.

M is for Motivation, which I get
    Lots of from my
    Teachers and parents
    Each and every day.

E is for Expectation, which I will
    Set high for myself
    To become a productive adult
    Helping others.

Victoria C.
DRAKE ELEMENTARY SCHOOL

Untitled

As time goes by I look back on my life,
My first bike ride to surfing my first tide.
From the boy next door
to working at the corner store.
As time goes by I look back on my life,
My first day at school to becoming cool.
From my first dance
To my first kiss with my best friend Lance.
As time goes by I look back on my life,
My first date to cutting the wedding cake.
From my first child
To having more that make me smile.

Gwendolyn S.
CHALMERS ELEMENTARY SCHOOL

Time Flies

Time flies like a human soul soaring.
Time flies like a hungry lion roaring.
Without time, life would be boring.

Time flies like a blow of the wind's breath.
Time flies like a cheetah hunting and doing his best.
Without time there would be endless rest.

Time will always pass by
Time will never die
And time will always fly.

Sharif K.
SOLOMON ELEMENTARY SCHOOL

Time

Time goes by
It flies in the sky
It's in the air
Blowing through your hair

It's not in a clock
All over the land
That goes tick-tock
With its little hand

Now that you have read this rhyme
about time
You know that time watches over us
with open arms.

Oscar C.
G. WASHINGTON ELEMENTARY SCHOOL

Time

Over time I see many places.
Over time I see many faces.
In time I see many days go by.
But through time I see the nice blue sky.
Time is like a river that goes slow and calm.
Time is like a bee buzzing fast around.
People say time comes and goes,
But I think time is just too slow.
So time, hurry up and go by,
'Cause I want to see the night sky.

Keelege E.
WEST PULLMAN ELEMENTARY SCHOOL

The Time Poem

Time can be so fast
When you're having a blast
Time can be so slow
When you are feeling low

Today will quickly turn into yesterday
Time speeds from Sunday to Saturday
Days, weeks, months, and years will soon all pass
Why is time oh so fast?

Lauren N.
ALCOTT ELEMENTARY SCHOOL

Time

Time flies according to us. I think it does fly too,
but it doesn't fly at all. Time never gets old, we get
old. Things that don't die live forever. Time is slow
and slurred. Time is wasteful. Time is wonderful. Time

can be annoying. Time is always left to us. Time never
dies; Time goes. Time is us. Time is god.
Time is irreversible.

Anonymous
SOLOMON ELEMENTARY SCHOOL

Time Waits for No One

You sit and wish you didn't feel your pain
Wondering if there's more for you to lose than for you to gain
As you sit and wonder why, time slowly passes you by
You sit and weep over unnecessary causes
But little do you know time never pauses
You lie around feeling sorry for yourself not doing anything
When you could be out living life doing many things
You cry yourself to sleep over and over again
Your broken heart is something only you and time can mend
You sit with tears in your eyes and watch the clock and as you notice
time has never stopped
Not for me, not for you, or anyone else
Take some time to get yourself together and do
what you have to get done
Because as you can see time waits for no one

Lacia S.
SCHILLER ELEMENTARY SCHOOL

Waiting

Waiting is hard
Waiting is the hardest
thing to master
to master waiting you
have to master
patience
to master patience
you have to know how

to wait
WAITING IS THE HARDEST THING TO DO

Ivan V.
PILSEN COMMUNITY ACADEMY

Untitled

Tick tock the time is up.
Is time to wake up.
The sun is bright it is
shining so nice in the big
blue sky. I wonder how it is to
be a clock staying up all night up.
I wish time will be up
so I don't have to be in the
school all day long.

Selene A.
BURBANK ELEMENTARY SCHOOL

School Time

7:00 waking up for school
8:00 getting ready for school
9:00 still in school; still in school
10:00 still in school; still in school
11:00 still in school; still in school
12:00 still in school; still in school
1:00 still in school; still in school
2:00 still in school; still in school
3:00 I'm free
    Halle lu jah!
        Yes! Yes! Yes!
            I'M FREE!

Kyla S.
DRAKE ELEMENTARY SCHOOL

There's Time

Time on the clock
Time on my watch
Time in the car
Time in my room
12:00 is coming soon
There's time in the kitchen
1:00 when I feed my chicken
There's time we should share
2:00 when I comb my hair
There's time over there
There's time everywhere!

Jervontae R.
DRAKE ELEMENTARY SCHOOL

How Time Passes

Time passes fast

I hate time.

More time equals more suffering
Everyone hates time
People hate time

When time passes people by
People get mad
Some like time,

some don't.

Everybody wants time to be over
So that's all about time.

Vahik
SOLOMON ELEMENTARY SCHOOL

What Does Time Predict in the Near Future?

What time what time
Do you predict?
What time what time
Do you see?
What time what time
Do you think and hear?

What time will we see warmth and kindness?
What will we touch and feel?
What time can we stop war and conflicts?
What time will we all stop the violence?
What time do we know?
And what time do we think?

What time what time
Does justice seek?
What time what time
Is it when all humans will become unique?

Irving J.
SMYTH ELEMENTARY SCHOOL

No More Time

What will happen with no time
Will you die or survive
How can you decide
With no more time

Will time
Still rhyme
Without a shrine
Or will that survive
With no more time

Alexis B.
BURROUGHS ELEMENTARY SCHOOL

Time

Time goes away and we
get older and older but if
time stopped we would stay younger and younger.
The time goes and we do not die young
but time goes and we get old.
We need time to get old and die.

Martin S.
PILSEN COMMUNITY ACADEMY

I Wish

I wish that I could go back in time
I wish that no one would have died
I wish that time could go slower
I wish that school was only 4 1/2 hours.

Tanaysia W.
SCHILLER ELEMENTARY SCHOOL

Dismissal Time

Ten more minutes until the bells rings,
Oh how I want to sing!

Today we did reading and math,
I can't wait to get in the bath!

We put our books in our sacks.
We took our coats from the racks.

It's dismissal time!

Five minutes to go,

We are all lined in a row.

The minutes are up.
I'm as happy as a pup.

When we get outside we play.
Hooray, it is the end of the day!

Amber C. and Shatyra W.
SMYTH ELEMENTARY SCHOOL

Untitled

Time goes slowly
We cannot wait to hit the door
We wait years and years
I feel like we never will be adults
The next day we are suddenly adults
We have bills to pay and speeches to say
Will hear what I say
We wish we could go back but we cannot
Time goes so quickly.

Joseph H.
KOZMINSKI COMMUNITY ACADEMY

Time

Time is what makes the world
Time is what makes people nervous
Time is patience
As time proceeds, people change.
Depending on what you are doing
Time's haste changes.
Growing older, time takes forever
But looking back, time takes a second

To come to your time.
Time is an important stage in the
circle of life.

Frank G.
SOLOMON ELEMENTARY SCHOOL

Decades

Deny
Everything and time
Can pass you like
Athletes in a
Decathlon taking
Every chance to
Shine

Zachary M.
CLAY ELEMENTARY SCHOOL

Time

Time to me is like someone eating a slice of cake
Which most of the time takes a long time to bake.
Time to me is like someone running a long mile
As the clouds pass by most of the time they make me smile.
Time to me is like money getting spent too fast
All of the time it does not even last.

Lashonda B.
CHALMERS ELEMENTARY SCHOOL

Time

Time flies by through and through.
It goes away and away and never comes back to us again.
Time is something to use, to waste, but when the end grows near,
You will hate it because you can't make it come back.
If time flew backwards the world would be weird.
It would be strange and messed up.
It would be gone.
Everything you know from the time you are in it
will be shattered and gone.
The time that we are in is the best so far.
Later when time has passed, you will pass on
to a new generation. To the future.

Jimmy T.
SOLOMON ELEMENTARY SCHOOL

Time Goes By

Once when I was strong
I could cut the trees among.
Now that I am weak I turned into an old freak.

Once I was told not to let the years go by
Now that I am old I only want to cry
For the years I let go by.

When I was young, I could run all day long
Now that I am old
Everything I try to do comes out wrong.

When I was young I had dreams that wanted to come true
Now I wait like a book to get due.

Daniel G.
PILSEN COMMUNITY ACADEMY

Is It My Time?

Will I be next
to close my eyes and take a last breath
Will it be me
Minutes from now able to be free
Will time flash by
Like a bolt of lightning
Leaving me helpless, so afraid, frightened
Will I wake up one day
Trying to say: Help Me
I'm scared, I don't know when it's my time to go
But who does know
All I want to know, is it my time
To go?

Kayla B.
CLAY ELEMENTARY SCHOOL

Infinity

Infinity
Slow, fast
Coming, going, slipping
It's on our hands
Time.

Tiffany B.
BURBANK ELEMENTARY SCHOOL

As Time Goes By

As time goes by you're just sitting
Wondering what will happen next
You're just sitting thinking I've made
It to see the next day, because

Things are changing, no it's people who
Change. I guess they're getting older
As time goes by, so remember to enjoy life
While you can because time does pass.

Deanna W.
KOZMINSKI COMMUNITY ACADEMY

Time

Time
Archaic infinite
Occurring passing lasting
Mostly taken for granted
Days

Stephany G.
BURBANK ELEMENTARY SCHOOL

Time

Day after day a flower grows.
It spreads its roots and stem out of its seedling.
    Week after week the roots grow
deeper and deeper into the soil.
    And then the stem grows up and out of the soil,
Like an angel flying out of heaven.
    .   Leaves glowing.
    After a month the petals begin to spread.
It grows older and older.
    And then, the flower
dies.

Emanuel C.
SOLOMON ELEMENTARY SCHOOL

Spring Time

When it is Spring time
I see many colors, flowers and birds.
The birds' song music to my ears.
I love the flowers.
The birds are beautiful.
The color of the birds is blue.
Some birds are brown.
The others are of different colors.
In spring, the flowers are so beautiful
and they smell good, very good.
I love to spend spring time watching the birds and flowers.

Melissa V.
BURBANK ELEMENTARY SCHOOL

Time

With time seasons change.
From the season of rain
to the season of snow.

After a cycle of four seasons
A year passes and we grow older...

Carlos F.
PILSEN COMMUNITY ACADEMY

Time

Too many years have passed
I watch my life go away
My young beauty that I once had has now faded
Everyday time flies by and by I wonder why?

Jazmin C.
CLAY ELEMENTARY SCHOOL

Out of Time, In Time

It's 1922 and I
Have just been built
By Lorado Taft who was inspired
By time and that is what I am: a piece of time.

It is 1942, two decades later
I still stand on, although my
Sculptor and dear friend does not
And as a sign of his sad passing the
Weather begins to become very dreary.

It is 1972, three more decades later
My friend has been gone 36 years now
And I start to chip away from weather bad
And this starts to make me feel very, very sad.

It is 2005, three decades, three years later
As my life goes on and on I become weary
Of how much time I have left, I am very leery
But what is this I see coming? Behold it is my saviors
These people of a different time come to help me of a time old.

Ryan K.
CLAY ELEMENTARY SCHOOL

The Fountain of Time

Every time I pass it, it stands out to me
Lorado Taft built this statue for us to see
I notice it almost twice a day
So there is not much for me to say
But if I could, I would say to you
It is all so very true
I have written this traditional rhyme
For I have seen the Fountain of Time.

Savion W.
KOZMINSKI COMMUNITY ACADEMY

The Art of Time

Time is everlasting,
it speaks to us, and
it affects us.
Important things in
time happen like the
makings of history's
landmarks. The people
who created it are
gone but their work
is still here. Frozen
in time. Time is expressed
in art, poetry, painting
and sculpturing.

Gaby P.
CHAVEZ ELEMENTARY SCHOOL

Sculpture

Paint is paint
Art is just art
A sculpture is people on your mind
You feel them on your head
You feel them on your skin
When you just discover that
they are passing you by
You want to feel them more
   You want a hug
   They run away
   But you want to follow them
   You keep on running
   You keep on following
   When you realize that they are dead.

Stephanie V.
PILSEN COMMUNITY ACADEMY

I Used to Be...

I used to be
strong.
Built for love
and time.

But, now
I'm falling
apart.
I'm not
noticed.

Can someone
make me feel
strong all over
again?

To show
young poets
that time
is
a part
of
life.

Aaron H.
MITCHELL ELEMENTARY SCHOOL

Fountain of Time

A shrine
Made of time
I call it mine
In all of this time

It has a father
But yet no mother

It has a sister
And maybe a brother

It's a fountain of time
It will last for all time
I call it mine
After all it is a fountain of time

Alexis B. and Crystal M.
BURROUGHS ELEMENTARY SCHOOL

Time Goes On

Time goes on by seconds
Time goes on by minutes
Time goes on by hours
Time goes on by years

Time goes on by seasons
Time goes on by spring
Time goes on by winter
Time goes on by fall

Time goes on by summer
Time goes on by time
Time goes quickly
Time goes fast and slowly

Esther G.
PILSEN COMMUNITY ACADEMY

Time

You fly by
leaving your mark
Aging people
I am 10 then
20 then 30

Father time you
seem old yet
You live
on like time
you stop
for
no one

Jonathan R.
DE DIEGO COMMUNITY ACADEMY

Time Goes

Time passes by
When you see a creature small
It will grow to something
you have never seen before.
Next time it's small,
then it is big.
But, it takes a year to grow bigger.
You think you'll stay small,
but you get big
And when you get big,
you'll turn small
Little by little.
When you are a 100 years old,
You will be no more.

Christopher O.
SOLOMON ELEMENTARY SCHOOL

Days

There are many days as you may know,
some go fast and others go slow,
and on those days I feel lazy or at least I think so,

maybe, maybe,
and sometimes I may feel as if I'm lapsing down a slope,
and I think to myself, is this a dream? nope nope,
but when I'm back in reality for a moment
it seems as if time has stood still or so it may seem
and I really feel crazy
it just might be the days,
maybe, maybe.

Derek P.
MOOS ELEMENTARY SCHOOL

Time

Time is unstoppable.
Time is time.
Time can be measured in seconds, minutes, hours,
days, months and years.
Time is a period of life we have in this world.
Time makes you get older till you die.
Time is an everyday tool.
Time varies from place to place.
Time has historical facts.
Time has adventurous events.
Time couldn't be heard but it could be seen in a watch or clock.
Time doesn't take up space.
Time is what many people need.
Time is daylight and night light.
Time can't be stopped.
Time evidently is unstoppable.

Gregoris S.
MOOS ELEMENTARY SCHOOL

Clock

Ticking tocking timing
The clock's hand
Timely
Went around in a circle

Lizzy Q.
ACOTT ELEMENTARY SCHOOL

Untitled

It's cool
When you get out of school
Tick tock tick tock
Goes the clock
When we get out
We scream and shout
But when I go home
I feel so alone
But day after day
Something was new
My cousin was born today
Hooray! Hooray!
So I'm not so alone
At home

Julian P.
G. WASHINGTON ELEMENTARY SCHOOL

Time with My Brother

My brother has been by my side since day one.
It was crazy, but we always had fun.
It was always us two, day in and day out.
I could depend on him without a doubt.

Once we played baseball, and broke a window.
We saw my aunt become a lonely widow.
When I was in need my brother was there for me.
We would always have a snowball fight in the winter
With my favorite cousin, we would always get her.
I've been in a lot of trouble.
He has been there in my struggles.
We would take like a big puzzle.
We would always put the pieces together.
He would always tell me that I'm getting older
And with each day a little bolder.
I'm happy he ain't a gangsta who pulls the trigger.
We've seen a lot of people come and go.
We've seen friends turn into foes,
But we've been together throughout our fear.
We've been together everytime we cried a tear.
And he's been my brother ever since.

Jovany C.
BURBANK ELEMENTARY SCHOOL

As Time Goes By

As time goes by
We watch our lives
Go by and by
We watch each day
As our time begins to fade away
We sit and listen as the sounds of our souls
Softly begin to drift away
As time goes by
we watch our lives
This is what happens
when our lives go by.

Phasia W.
KOZMINSKI COMMUNITY ACADEMY

El Tiempo del Amor

El tiempo del amor que siento yo por ti.
El tiempo es algo relacionado a ti.
El dia cuando se acabe el tiempo no se
que haría yo si tu no estás aquí.
El tiempo es la luz que me acerca mas a ti,
el dia del anonchecer.
El dia de mañana tu contaras conmigo
para que no se acabe el tiempo.

Anonymous
CLAY ELEMENTARY SCHOOL

The Time for Love

The time for love that I feel for you.
Time is something related to you.
The day when time runs out I don't know
what I would do if you were not here.
Time is the light that brings me closer to you,
when the day gets dark.
The day of tomorrow you will count on me
for time not to run out.

Translation by Nancy Diaz and Jeanette Alfaro

Time

Time makes us grow
Time helps us learn
Time is history
For us to know
We have all this time to see
And hear, don't waste all your
Time sitting in chairs.

Yaritza M.
MOOS ELEMENTARY SCHOOL

Students respond to Zahara Baker.

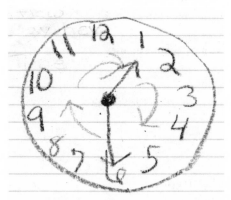

Kacy H.
SOLOMON ELEMENTARY SCHOOL

Frank G.
SOLOMON ELEMENTARY SCHOOL

I had a clock.
sThat told the time.
It was hidden in
my sock. And It was
colored lime.

by Teanna J.
Room 211

Teanna J.
BURBANK ELEMENTARY SCHOOL

Students recite "Jane Addams" by Gwendolyn Brooks.

I Remember

I remember going to Pope School
I remember being cool
I remember my best friends
I remember happiness that never ends
I remember running wild
I remember being a child
I remember me

Darnell S.
POPE ELEMENTARY SCHOOL

I Used to Be a Kid with No Worries

I used to be a kid with no worries
But now I feel the world moving
And time passing by.
I was a child with no worries.
Now I'm scared of time.
I could see worries and problems me having.
I worry about me at the year
2080 when I'm old, an elderly man.
I used to be a kid with no worries
But now I feel the world
Moving and time passing by.

Eduardo C.
MITCHELL ELEMENTARY SCHOOL

Time

Time has a long lifetime
It has more decades to go than the worth of a dime
We fly through time like we pass signs on the expressway
But sometimes it's slow I say
It's slow when you're waiting for something
Even though time has its ways of making you sad, mad
Or sometimes even glad
It is what we survive on
If no time we would be gone
Time is when dinosaurs were heard to roam
Time was when 9/11's terrorists
through the building seemed to comb
Time is yet to be, time stays, we don't, people will see
Time is yet to be when it is 2024
But until my time is gone, I will enjoy it and maybe even soar.

Jacqui
G. WASHINGTON ELEMENTARY SCHOOL

Present

I always said that
There's no time like the present,
This was my saying.

This is what I think.
There is no time like my time
And I will not sink.

I will say this once:
The present is the best time,
For a child to be. . .

Ashley C.
WHITE ELEMENTARY SCHOOL

Time

Time is then, time is now, and time is yet to come. As the rain turns into snow; and as the wind will not blow. Time will not stop. Time is a memory good or bad, funny or sad. Time is a good thing to have. Use every second, minute, hour, day, week, month, and year the best way you can.

Vianca R.
KOZMINSKI COMMUNITY ACADEMY

How Long Do I Have?

My childhood
was great but
when I was little
I always wanted to be an adult

I'm 25 now and as I
watch kids play I
say that used to
be me

Years have passed
now I'm 79 it's
not long

until my skin
has dried up

now I rest
peacefully
in my grave

looking back
as I was one to
this very day.

Joseph L.
MITCHELL ELEMENTARY SCHOOL

Time Can Come and Go

Time can come and go,
Time cannot stay, oh no!
We are just a piece of time,
Time cannot rewind.
Some people think time is slow,
Time is not that slow no, no.

Alex G.
KOZMINSKI COMMUNITY ACADEMY

Time Passes By

Some people say "time is not fair"
Others say time is a gift
To me time is valuable
You must use it wisely
Because it may pass quickly

Time is constant
We're the ones that pass by
What we do with it is part of our future
Time is given to you
In hopes of you using it wisely

Elders are aware of time passing by
While kids just want to have fun
Teachers and parents say "kids are our future"
But the truth is,
Time gives us a future.

Estephany A.
CLAY ELEMENTARY SCHOOL

As Time Passes By

As time goes by you don't know what to do.
As soon as you think you are still the same age,
Time passes you by.
As soon as you think you are grown,
Time passes you by.
When the times go you don't know what to do
because time has already passed you by.
As I get older I wish time would start all over again.

Ebony W.
KOZMINSKI COMMUNITY ACADEMY

Time and Memories

Points of view never change,
my mother thinks I'm her baby,
but I'm almost 12.

I can't change the way
my mother sees me.
Each day I get older,
and older.
But memories stay.

My mother wants to go back,
so she can have a second childhood.
But now we are older,
and have more things to do.

People change,
but things stay the same.
Mothers care for us,
and don't want us to go,
but life goes on,
and we have to move on.

But memories always stay,
and as long as you remember
your love will never change.

Janette T.
MITCHELL ELEMENTARY SCHOOL

Poem of Time

We go to a place
A place where time doesn't exist.
We travel in space
Where there's unlimited time all around.
There are only two places in the universe where time exists
Where human life exists is the first
And the second is where we will never travel to.

Matthew M.
SOLOMON ELEMENTARY SCHOOL

Clocks

Time is just seconds, minutes, and hours.
But if there was no time, that would be great.
We would all be late for school, and they would
accidentally let us all go home early.
The bus driver would be late and we would have
time to play, but, it would be bad because
I wouldn't know when wrestling was on.
Having no time could be good and bad.

Jonathan G.
SOLOMON ELEMENTARY SCHOOL

Time Stay

Time goes slow and fast
Don't know what I would do without you time
I would never be late to a debate for class president.
Time oh time stay and don't go fast.
I want to be late
so stay.

Charlie M.
PILSEN COMMUNITY ACADEMY

Time, Time, Time

Please don't go
Time, Time, Time
Please take away the rain, sleet and snow
Time, Time, Time
I will look at my digital watch and hopefully you will
make the numbers slow
Time, Time, Time
Please make the sun show
Time, Time, Time
Please make my wishes so

DeVontre S.
KOZMINSKI COMMUNITY ACADEMY

Untitled

I can't wait for summer
all my days seem funner

I can't wait till 2:38
So I can hop the tall gate

I can't wait for the teacher
My handwriting keeps getting neater

I can't wait for the flowers
So I can punch all the cowards

I can't wait to play my game
So I can make it to the hall of fame

I can't wait to climb the hill
When my mom pays her bills

Yep I can't wait

Travis A.
SCHILLER ELEMENTARY SCHOOL

Time Is Not Still

Time is not still
    As you get up or
Lie down

Time will still go on
    Like a heartbeat
Time is not made of gold
Time is never to be stolen

Time is wasted,
    Can never be saved
You just have to be
    PATIENT!

Libra W.
DRAKE ELEMENTARY SCHOOL

Time Already Past

When the time of the
time that you have
been waiting for doesn't
come, you think it is so
far but time is fast.
It will soon come and pass.

You might see it from
two years and on, but next
day you wake up and end
up knowing that those two
years already passed.

Aurora V.
CHAVEZ ELEMENTARY SCHOOL

Time Line

Time, like a line
It begins, doesn't end.
Time has history, the future a mystery
Time never up, it feels like the clock is stuck
Time is mine, even when it rains
Even when it shines.

Time like a line
It begins, doesn't end.
Time plays with your mind, fast forwards and rewinds
Time line take time, year after year
Time after time.

Time like a line
It begins but doesn't end.
Time goes fast, time goes slow.
Time is like a car, time is like a boat.

William M.
CHAVEZ ELEMENTARY SCHOOL

The Times

Looking at the time
Hoping it'll fly by
When will dis day end?
Looking at the clock
Tick tock tick tock
Watching seconds go by
The day seems like it'll never finish
Suffocating just waiting
For dis day to end
Tired of dis drama
Tired of all dis war
Tired of people bringing themselves
Or other people down
Making people frown
Tick tock tick tock
My head's going in swirls
As the world twirls
Around and around
My head spins
Thinkin' bout all them sins
I'm tired and
The clock is still ticking
Tick tock tick tock
Reminiscin' all dem times
Wonderin' why god made things happen
Love . . . life . . . cries . . . lies . . . tears . . . and all deez years . . .
All deez back-stabbers, cheaters, players and deceivers
Tick tock tick tock
Still waiting for dis day to end "when, when?"
As the sun comes down
My head still stuck with questions
My mind still stuck with suggestions
My eyes still stuffed with cries
As I begin to lie down
I cry myself to sleep
Thinkin' bout all deez years I been living
All deez years I fell in love
And all deez years I been hurt

All deez years I been heartbroken
I've learned lessons throughout these past 12 years
And so I hear
The clock still go
Tick tock tick tock

Tani C.
MOOS ELEMENTARY SCHOOL

Time

They say time heals all wounds
I'm not sure that this is true.
Time flies by without you even noticing
what you went through.
Sometimes time goes by so fast
you don't even remember the bad things in the past.
Sometimes you think it erases all your blues, and it does.
You mostly never have a lot of clues
for what you been through.
Time, they say time heals all wounds,
And now I know that this is true.

Crystal S.
MOOS ELEMENTARY SCHOOL

In Between Time

Time is very priceless.
When you lose a loved one
You have to carry on.

Time is very precious
When you have a loved one
You never want them to go.

Time is everywhere.
It is like a friend.
The friendship never ends.
Time never stops for a break.
Time is everywhere.

Sommer J.
WEST PULLMAN ELEMENTARY SCHOOL

Remembering Me

Me
Remembering
I used to drink out of a bottle.
I grow
time flies
but I'm still me.

Communicating is hard.
Soon I turn older,
my body changes
more problems arrive.

I grow
like a seed grows.
I grow,
I soon get a job
that will carry me on.
I will soon just be an adult,
then I'll get to be old.

I take a deep breath
and I'm ready
to go.

Genesis P.
MITCHELL ELEMENTARY SCHOOL

Haiku

Watching the clouds fly,
They change every second,
Swiftly moving free.

Derek L.
TRUMBULL ELEMENTARY SCHOOL

Time

Time was invented
to change things
or have a second chance
in what you did
wrong.

That is what time
is all about,
taking time
or having a second chance.

Jesus B.
MITCHELL ELEMENTARY SCHOOL

Time

As I speak time
Flows
When I think the wind
Blows.
But time still goes on and on.
Sometimes I wish time would slow down.
Sometimes I wish time would go fast.
But life is short and I would like to live every moment
Of it

That's why I like time.

Steve W.
KOZMINSKI COMMUNITY ACADEMY

Time Flies by So Quickly When I'm with My Family

Time goes by
so quickly
here with my family

having some fun
at the barbe-Q
talking and playing

Me and my cousins are playing double dutch
until the food
is all done
we're having ribs and spaghetti
with meat balls and mash potatoes

I'm just so excited
but time flies
by so quickly

It's almost dark
I don't want time to pass by
so quickly
because I'm having so much fun
with my family

Desiree H.
MITCHELL ELEMENTARY SCHOOL

Time

Time is a thing
That no one in the world
Can stop

Time is when
You start to develop &
When you start
Getting too big
For your clothes

Time is a very
Precious thing
It can be used foolishly
And
Time can be used wisely

Kyaah E.
DRAKE ELEMENTARY SCHOOL

Time

Flowing, passing, going
The time
Continuously
Flows

Jacoby M.
ALCOTT ELEMENTARY SCHOOL

Time Poem

Time is like a game, a monopoly running our lives.
The rules cannot be changed, or altered, nor can it mold
and change from its original lines.

Is there any beginning, where does it end,
Was it created before existence, and who creates
its manipulating bends.

Many wise men have said that it is among the seven things
from above man's reach.
I think that it is a man himself playing and taunting, trying to teach.

Can man change its direction, can he wield its power and strength,
Can a man ever be its master, can he control its sense.

It is an ever running force. A force that creates great skillful
consequences and results.
It is beyond our imagination and above our many defaults.

Time is me, time is you, time is everything around.
It cannot be illustrated or demonstrated but it can be found.

Miraj S.
ALCOTT ELEMENTARY SCHOOL

I Wish

I wish I had the time to wish what I want in life
I wish I had the time to not be hateful
I wish I had the time to think about getting into high school
I wish I had the time to think about summer
I wish I had the time to think about the minutes of time
I wish I had the time to stop wishing for time

Shimanda C.
SCHILLER ELEMENTARY SCHOOL

Waiting

I've been waiting for you, while time has vanished
 Wishing that you would come is leaving me in full depression.
Wanting you so bad, longing for something I never had
 You got something old come get something new
Letting you go is something that I can't do.
 As time go slow,
I want to be with you that's something I know.
 Acting like you belong to me,
While time is passing rapidly.
 While I'm wasting my time hoping you will be mine soon.
But the only thing I can do is keep waiting on you.

Ronnica A.
SCHILLER ELEMENTARY SCHOOL

Wasting Time

Fighting, Sad
Sitting, Playing, Acting Up
Mad, Crazy, boring
Friend

Bobby M.
SCHILLER ELEMENTARY SCHOOL

Time

Time is a good friend of mine
he flies and flies.

Time, oh time when
will you ever pass
by.

You're my old friend
since the beginning of
time.

Time is my friend
and when we part
It's not goodbye.

For time can fly
and so can I.

Marc C.
DE DIEGO COMMUNITY ACADEMY

Time Goes On

Time is a walking shadow
That walks on without a person
Time does not wait
It decides your fate

Time is a never ending runner
That never gets old
We get old
It all goes on

Time is as forever as infinity
Enjoy your time and read this rhyme
So you will find that
Time goes on.

Luis S.
G. WASHINGTON ELEMENTARY SCHOOL

Time Passes Quickly

It feels like it was just yesterday.
When I was a little boy
Playing with my friends
I never cared of time.

Sometimes bad things happen over time
Like the time my uncle passed away
Good things happen too
When we see the light.

I feel like just last night
My sister finished school
Or the first time I went to school
Or the last time I saw my dad.

Or the time I moved to a new school.
The time my sister was born.
I still remember my oldest sister in 7th grade
Now she is 20 and has a baby.

People pass away
And babies are born
This is the cycle of time
we all join in.

Jose G.
CLAY ELEMENTARY SCHOOL

Time

Memories will last forever, but people do not.
The letters you wrote will last forever, but people do not.
The action you took will last forever, but people do not.
The photos that were taken will last forever, but people will not.
The seasons will come and last forever, but people do not.
The people you see today will go.

The earth you once walked on will still be here.

Tynisha D.
POPE ELEMENTARY SCHOOL

Time

Time is one of a kind.
There's a time when you are born.
There's a time when you start to walk.
There's a time when you start school.
There's a time when you graduate.
There's a time when you fall in love.
There's a time when you get married.
And there's a time when it happens again and again.
Time is one of a kind.
The time never recovers.
Don't waste it!

Ixtlily E.
G. WASHINGTON ELEMENTARY SCHOOL

Movements of Time

Time is slow.
It creeps by and
you will never know.

Time is fast.
It roars by and
will always last.

I can catch time,
and then I can't
because the motion of
time is slow and fast.

Jakalah B.
WEST PULLMAN ELEMENTARY SCHOOL

Time-a-Mania

Time is like a breeze,
It flies like an angel.
It is very long.

Krupa P.
SOLOMON ELEMENTARY SCHOOL

Flock of Birds

I saw,
a flock of birds.
Singing,
and talking.
Flying around,
the nice fresh wind,
and the sun,
saying to the birds,
I'm back.
The birds
feel
as if they
were in Acapulco,
when they are
in the United States.
In eight more months,
the birdies will fly,
away,
until the sun says,
I'm back!

Alex P.
MITCHELL ELEMENTARY SCHOOL

Las Cuatro Estaciones

Primavera es una estación del ano
En la que todas las plantas
Y los arboles reverdecen
Y se ven muy bien.
Verano: en el verano la temperatura
Es muy caliente, el sol brilla mucho.
Es la estación en la que la gente va al parque.
Otoño: la estación en la que
Las hojas se caen de los arboles,
El calor se comiensa a alejar.
Inveirno hace mucho frio.

Jose M.
CLAY ELEMENTARY SCHOOL

The Four Seasons

Spring is a season of the year
In which all the plants
And trees bloom
And it looks very nice.
Summer: in the summer the temperature
Is very hot, the sun shines a lot,
It's the season when people go to the park.
Autumn: the season in which
the leaves fall from the trees,
and the heat begins to fade.
Winter is very cold.

Translation by Nancy Diaz and Jeanette Alfaro

Time Goes By

Time goes slow,
Time goes fast,
Time goes forward in the fall,
Time goes backward in the spring,
Time is changing everything,
All through the months, years go by,
Time changes and so do I.

Kristina B.
BURBANK ELEMENTARY SCHOOL

Slow and Fast Time

Time so slow. You want to be
                    18 but it
goes so slow.
You want to drive
                    but time goes
                    too slow. But
                    when you're
                    10 or 11 you
                    become 12 or 13
so fast. Why can't age go fast when
you're little and slow when you're big?
                    so you can get
                    a house, and not be
controlled by your parents. When you
                    are in school
                    it goes slow and fast.
When you are outside it
goes fast.
Why can't time go by fast
when you want something? There is
time to go, and hours, and minutes, and
seconds never stopping.

Jesus G.
CHAVEZ ELEMENTARY SCHOOL

The Past and the Future

Time is short.
It seems like my clock has stopped
when I look at my watch.
I look through distance far and near.
It seems like it's taking all darn year.
All darn year just for my age to pass,
Just as fast as the days pass.
It's telling me to slow down,
And look back into history.
See how much I'm learning day and evening.
As much as I play the game,
I need to know that things will remain the same.
I wake up in the morning very, very early.
As I did not know the importance of death.
So important for a person with very much wealth.
As always, I'm late for school.
Now I have to review
The things that happened in 2002.
I'm quick to learn about my ancient ancestors,
Then I turn on the radio and listen to new records.

Although it sounds like a rhyme,
I'm just telling you a poem about time.

Jermaine F.
SCHILLER ELEMENTARY SCHOOL

Time is Everywhere

At a certain time they signed the Declaration
Of Independence.
But "time" is the key word in that particular sentence.
And if there's a key then there must be a lock,
So time is even the key to 12 o'clock.
It's the second, it's the moment, it's the hours, it's the days.
It's the sections, through the stone-age, it's in the clock now they say.

It's on their wrist, it exists, it's irresistible to some.
People wonder if time is numbers from infinity down to one.
Time is here, time is there, time is really all around;
Time appears to be rare, but time is everywhere to be found.

Darronte M.
SMYTH ELEMENTARY SCHOOL

Time

Time goes right past your eyes
It's so fast you won't realize
There are many things from the past,
I can't believe they go by so fast.
There is always a mystery
And it is from history.

Timothy S.
ROGERS ELEMENTARY SCHOOL

What Is Time?

What is time?
You can't make it,
You can't break it

What is time?
Don't take it for granted,
This may be all you have

What is time?
Any day can be your last,
Time goes by fast

What is time?
You'll never know what happens next,
Until you live your past

What is time?
That's your opinion
Not mine.

Ashley S.
CLAY ELEMENTARY SCHOOL

Time O' Time

One day you will realize that life waits on no one but itself
Soon you will have to realize that it is time to think about your future
    not time.
It's not like a walk in the park with birds singing and kids are playing.
But time will come and these things will be crowding you
and all you can do is try to take advantage of this time
and love every minute of it and it will be okay.
So just take every chance you can get.
Just remember that some days you will cry some days you will laugh.
Always remember to enjoy life as it lasts and think positive
and don't always think sad things
and try to bring happiness to your life.

Jakia D.
KOZMINSKI COMMUNITY ACADEMY

Time

Time
Nostalgic, Revealing
Passing, Arriving, Coming
Perched amongst our minds
Destiny

Cristina G.
BURBANK ELEMENTARY SCHOOL

Precious Time Forever

Time is precious,
We must save the time we have left.
There are things to be done,
Things to be said.

Time goes by fast, time goes by slow.
Some people are young, some begin to get old.

Time is like a blooming flower,
Full of youth and full of sorrow.
Time is full of surprises,
Being curious for the next tomorrow.

Time is full of weather,
sun, snow, sleet or rain.
But even if we're not here,
It'll always stay the same.

Time goes on forever,
like a spinning top.
Time goes on forever,
until your top stops.

Nettali S.
CHAVEZ ELEMENTARY SCHOOL

Time Flies By

Time flies by
Once I was a baby
Now I am all grown
Time flies by
Once I was all grown
Now I am old
Now it is time to say goodbye

But time still flies by.

Anthony S.
ROGERS ELEMENTARY SCHOOL

It's Time It's Time

It's time It's time
>   Well what can I say
It's time It's time
>   We grow older every day
It's time It's time
>   We see the world we have to face
It's time It's time
>   And we have none to waste
It's time It's time
>   To go out and play
It's time It's time
>   Everyone say
It's time It's time
>   To do things the right way
It's time It's time
>   For everyone to come out and say
It's time It's time

Quinesha H.
SMYTH ELEMENTARY SCHOOL

Time

Time is clear as glass.
It tastes like nothing.
It sounds like kids playing.
When I think of it I think of someone aging before my eyes.
It doesn't feel like anything.

Deving B.
ALCOTT ELEMENTARY SCHOOL

What Is Time?

What is time?
Where is time?
Does it go fast
Or does it go slow?

Is time over here?
Is time over there?
Or is time everywhere?

Is it in the city?
Is it in the country?
Or is time everywhere?

Tick tock, where are you?
I'm ready for that right time
To come.
Hooray 2:45 is finally here!

There goes 3:00,
Here comes 4:00.
Time just walked in
And out the door.

Christian H.
DRAKE ELEMENTARY SCHOOL

Time

Time goes by fast.
It feels like it never lasts.
Time passes right before your eyes,
you really don't know why it goes by that quick.
A minute might feel like a century
but, then again an hour might feel like a minute.
You want more time,
more time to do things you haven't done.

Time to enjoy fun
or just to spend with the ones you love.
Before you know it your time is up.
You don't want it to ever end.
So, it's better to take advantage
of the time you have left.
Meet the people you haven't met,
sing the songs you haven't sung,
walk the steps you haven't walked,
do the things you haven't done.
Enjoy the time you have,
don't let it go to waste;
before it is too late.

Stephany M.
KILMER ELEMENTARY SCHOOL

As Time Pass By

As time pass by
We sit and listen to the things
In our lives
We watch each day
Go by and by
We listen as our minds wander
Away and away
As our time goes running by and by
We watch carefully as our time
And our lives go fading away
As times pass by
We sit and listen to the things
In our lives.

Rayvin C.
KOZMINSKI COMMUNITY ACADEMY

The Dog that Took Over

I used to be the baby
but then my dog took over.
Since we got the dog
things have changed.
My mom bought him a lot of things
haircuts, food, treats, toys and treatments.
I used to feel sad
but now I do not because I have the dog
to play with and lie with.

Deidre H.
MITCHELL ELEMENTARY SCHOOL

A Cat's Life

Time goes by cat
Year by year cat you sit on the rug
You used to catch rats
Now you sit on the rug
You're getting older cat
Year by year
You used to be my light orange cat
Not you're dirty orange
You finally curled up into a ball
By the fire
The end has come

Brittany C.
G. WASHINGTON ELEMENTARY SCHOOL

I Can Wait

Time
is one thing
I can wait to
go by.

Why?
Because
as time goes
I begin to grow
not young
but old.

With wrinkles
on my face
my hair is no longer
shiny black
but a gray fog.

Yes I can wait
for time to go by.

Because I am not yet
ready to lie down
and go.

Yaritza A.
MITCHELL ELEMENTARY SCHOOL

Future

In the old days
You had to do things manually
But nowadays
You have to do things simultaneously.
I lay my head back and think about the future
I wonder if the future is going to be super.

Collis R.
POPE ELEMENTARY SCHOOL

AFTERWORD

I want to congratulate everyone who participated in Time for Poetry. Every aspect of this program made me proud to be a Chicagoan and to be a part of this project.

Over two thousand poems were written about the *Fountain of Time* by Chicago school children. These poems exemplify a depth of feeling and a talent for words that is extraordinary. The results are also a great credit to the teachers who participated in the program, as well as the Poetry Foundation.

I hope all the students will fondly remember the day they recited poems next to the *Fountain of Time*. This sculpture is one of Chicago's great treasures. Lorado Taft, the Chicago sculptor who created it, is recognized as one of the premier late-19th-century, early-20th-century artists in America.

We are so lucky to have not only the *Fountain of Time* but also more than one hundred great sculptures in our parks. Chicago's collection of outdoor sculpture is recognized as the finest in America and the reason we began Time for Poetry was not only to celebrate Chicago poets but to call attention to the treasure trove of sculpture in our parks.

I hope that everyone who participated in this program will continue to have a great admiration for these works of art, as well as a sense of responsibility for maintaining them. Both poetry and sculptures are part of the artistic tradition that exemplifies the finest in human spirit. I hope that each of you—students, parents, and teachers—will carry a part of Time for Poety with you for years to come and that you will always treasure the arts for what they give to all of us.

CINDY MITCHELL
COMMISSIONER
CHICAGO PARK DISTRICT